From Darkness into LIGHT

Dennis Wrigley

Artwork by
Christine Garwood

From Darkness into Light

Facing human unhappiness

Published and distributed by The Maranatha Community Trust,
102 Irlam Road, Flixton, Manchester M41 6JT
Tel: 0161 748 4858 Fax: 0161 747 7379
www.maranathacommunity.org.uk
email: info@maranathacommunity.org.uk

ISBN : 978-0-9565717-1-7

Printed in the United Kingdom

From Darkness into Light

Facing human unhappiness

Contents

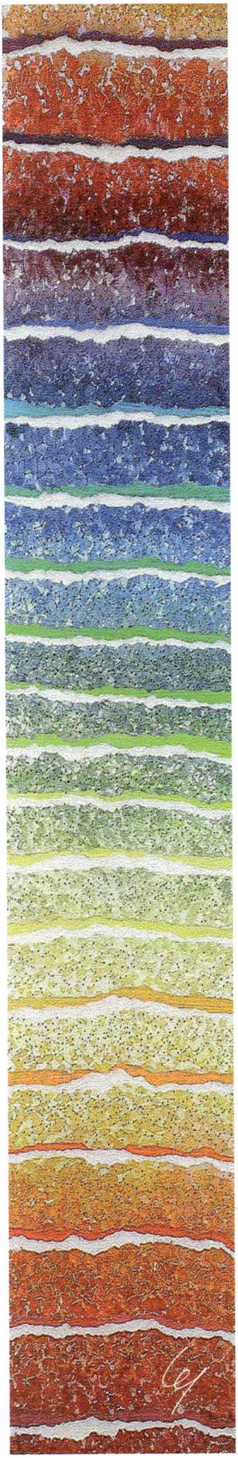

Shine in my darkness, Lord
dispel the doubt and fear
that cling so close.
Turn the weak moonlight of my faith
to brighter day
in which I see your radiance,
know your love.

Eddie Askew

From Darkness into Light

Facing human unhappiness

Foreword

Many people struggle with great unhappiness at some stage in their life. These words acknowledge the reality of the darkness encountered but affirm the reality of God's love which is revealed in darkness. These reflections, thoughts and prayers start with our immediate situation and frequently lead us to the Cross. It is hoped that they will bring comfort and healing as God leads us out of our darkness into His light.

In facing up to human unhappiness, it is hoped that this book will be a contribution to healing those who are in need and lead to the discovery of the immediate and real presence of God. This book is rooted in a broad range of Christian tradition and is commended by an Anglican Vicar, a Roman Catholic Priest and a United Reformed Church Minister.

"When life is dark and your heart is heavy, there are two possible ways to pray. One is to look up at the face of God and hope that something of His goodness and beauty and truth and love will come down and infiltrate your situation. However, this is not always possible. We may look up but see nothing. Between our darkness and God's light there may be an apparently impenetrable cloud. So the other way to pray is to face the darkness, own the darkness, and offer that darkness to the God whom for the time being we cannot see at all. For if God is God, He will find His own way of breaking through to us. It is this second way of prayer that Dennis Wrigley offers us in his brilliant book, 'From Darkness into Light'. Small in size it may be, but its potential for healing is immense. For it shows that within the Gospel there are elements which can meet us at our every point of need and in meeting us can bring us the healing touch of Jesus. Thank you, Dennis. We are all in your debt."

Canon Roy Lawrence

"There is a great hunger for the Word of God in our time and place and spiritual malnutrition is a fact of life in the midst of deep human suffering. This inspired work will bring consolation, healing and reassurance to those searching for the face of God in a secular-humanist society. 'From Darkness into Light' conveys the great treasure of Christian faith in beautiful words of compassion and hope and will touch many lives. I am privileged to endorse it".

Father William Keogh

"In these prayers raw experience encounters resolute and buoyant faith, while interweaving Bible passages provide a sure foundation of support. 'From Darkness into Light' will sustain and encourage any who are battling with their own times of darkness".

Rev. Hazel Catton

Introduction

The world is bursting with sorrow.
This vale of tears contains
the groans and cries of despair
of vast numbers
who know deep within them
the searing pain
the agonising distress
the tragedy beyond all words
the unanswered questions
the silence beyond silence
the darkness beyond darkness
the place of brokenness
the place
where hope has shrivelled up
and died.

As we face disaster
in our lives
God draws us
near to the Cross.
There is no pain
He has not borne
there is no sorrow
He does not know
there are no tears
He has not shed.

He comes
not to explain
but to share
and love.

In Him
we are more than conquerors.

*"I will not leave you as orphans, I will come to you…
because I live, you also will live."
(John 14.18-19)*

Darkness

The deep darkness
which overwhelms
my being
casting its
dark shadows
over every thought
and feeling
is known
and is felt
by You my Lord.

Upon Your Cross

You bear and share
the sharp
penetrating pain
which wracks
every part of me.
The agony and sorrow
which is
beyond all words,
deep
within my being,
is owned by You.
The tears I shed
flow freely
down Your cheeks.

Cast down
and crushed
I lift my gaze
and see You
bearing
all human despair and ugliness
all broken heartedness and sorrow.

Lead me, Lord
to the place
where I am safely held
and embraced
by You.

In Your crucified
brokenness
open my eyes
to see that
Your limitless love
is, even now
transforming
black darkness into light,
terrible defeat into victory,
that in my weakness
I may triumph
in Your Cross
which towers
over all
the wrecks of time
and human frailty
bringing the depths of peace
to troubled souls
and healing
to all sickness
and despair.

"The light shines in the darkness and the darkness did not overcome it."(John 1.5) NRSV

"If I say 'Surely the darkness will hide me and the light become night around me, even the darkness will not be dark to you...'" (Ps. 139.11-12)

"Though I have fallen, I will rise. Though I sit in darkness the Lord will be my light." (Micah 7.8)

"From the sixth hour until the ninth hour darkness came over all the land." (Matt. 27.45)

"He was in the world, and though the world was made through him, the world did not recognize him. He came to that which was his own, but his own did not receive him." (John 1.10,11)

"The Lord is my light and my salvation – whom shall I fear? The Lord is the stronghold of my life – of whom shall I be afraid?" (Ps. 27.1)

"God is light and in him there is no darkness at all." (1 Jn. 1.5)

"I have come into the world as a light, so that no-one who believes in me should stay in darkness." (Jn. 12.46)

"Let the light of your face shine upon us." (Ps. 4.6)

"God who said 'Let light shine out of darkness', made his light shine in our hearts to give us the light of the knowledge of the glory of God in the face of Christ." (2 Cor. 4.6)

"My God turns my darkness into light." (Ps. 18.28)

Fear

Fear stalks our lives
corrodes our souls
assaults our innermost beings.
Fear destroys foundations,
steals security.
Fear causes us to tremble about the future
and to be torn apart by the present.
Fear invades us as a disease
twisting our judgement,
fooling our hearing,
distorting our seeing.

Fear breeds doubt and dismay.
I am no longer safe.
I am no longer secure.
I become afraid
of the darkness of the past,
the darkness of the present
and the darkness of what will be.
And in the darkness of this fear
I stumble and fall,
my heart grows hard and cold,
I lose all hope, all joy.

Yet the penetrating, sharp
and bright light of love
can enter this darkness and transform it.
The perfect love of Christ
casts out all fear, chasing the shadows away,
claiming life in place of death,
claiming joy in place of despair,
claiming laughter in place of tears,
claiming peace in place of turmoil.

Am I prepared to allow His light, His love,
to sweep away all fear of darkness,
dying and death from within my soul?
Am I prepared to hear, receive and believe
the words of the one who made me,
who loves me and saves me? - *"Do not be afraid"*.

Am I prepared to believe and trust Him when He promises me that His presence is with me and within me and that He will never, ever, leave or forsake me?

You will give me the faith
to entrust my days and nights,
my months and years
and all eternity to Your safe-keeping,
that I may say "I am not afraid".

"Do not be afraid, little flock, for your Father has been pleased to give you the kingdom." (Lk 12.32)

"There is no fear in love. But perfect love drives out fear, because fear has to do with punishment. The one who fears is not made perfect in love." (1 Jn. 4.18)

"Have no fear of sudden disaster or of the ruin that overtakes the wicked..." (Prov. 3.25)

"He who dwells in the shelter of the Most High will rest in the shadow of the Almighty. I will say of the Lord, 'He is my refuge and my fortress, my God, in whom I trust'." (Ps. 91.1-2)

"I sought the Lord, and he answered me: he delivered me from all my fears." (Ps. 34.4)

"The Lord is my helper; I will not be afraid." (Heb.13.6)

"Do not be afraid for I am with you. "(Is. 43.5)

"I am the light of the world." (Jn. 8.12)

"God is our refuge and strength, an ever-present help in trouble. Therefore we will not fear, though the earth give way and the mountains fall into the heart of the sea, though its waters roar and foam and the mountains quake with their surging." (Ps. 46.1-3.)

Insecurity

I yearn for safety.
I demand protection from the dangers
of an unknown future.
Deep down, whatever preparations,
I know I am vulnerable to all manner of
situations, unforeseen and unexpected.

I know a world which is insecure
and in my own insecurity I know
that nothing is permanent,
that the foundations of my life
are constantly at risk.

For a time I may believe
the false prophets and deny the dangers
but the truth soon comes rushing into me
so that I am unable to build
the secure wall of protection around me
without which my very foundations are at risk.

Yet the truth which God proclaims to me
is that my weakness can be made strength,
that I can lie down and sleep in peace,
knowing that the name of the Lord
is a strong tower.

In the day of trouble
You will keep me safe in Your dwelling
and You will set my feet upon a rock.
In You, Lord, I can take refuge.

"You will be secure, because there is hope; you will look about you and take your rest in safety." (Job 11.18)

"In you, O Lord, I have taken refuge..." (Ps. 71.1)

"He alone is my rock and my salvation; he is my fortress, I shall not be shaken." (Ps. 62.6)

"Blessed is the man who trusts in the Lord, whose confidence is in him. He will be like a tree planted by the water that sends out its roots by the stream. It does not fear when heat comes; its leaves are always green. It has no worries in a year of drought and never fails to bear fruit." (Jer. 17.7-8)

"The Lord will be your confidence and will keep your foot from being snared." (Prov. 3. 26)

"In all your ways acknowledge him, and he will make your paths straight." (Prov. 3.6)

"I can do everything through him who gives me strength." (Phil 4.13)

"Everything is possible for him who believes." (Mk. 9.23)

"Cast all your anxiety on him because he cares for you." (1 Peter 5.7)

"The Lord has become my fortress, and my God the rock in whom I take refuge." (Ps. 94.22)

"He is my stronghold, my refuge and my saviour." (2 Sam. 22.3)

"Your Father knows what you need before you ask him." (Matt. 6.8)

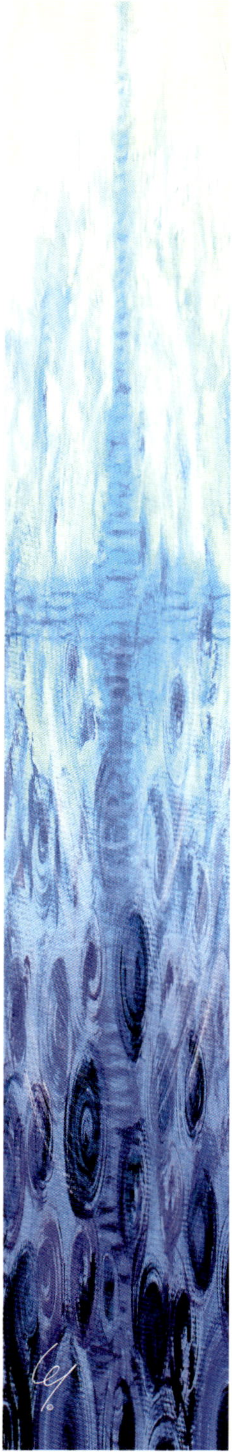

Hopelessness

Everything seemed so sure and certain,
sound and safe
yet the fierce storm has blown,
destroying,
sweeping away
all that seemed of value to me.
I gasp for breath as I struggle
in the swirling waters,
a flood-tide overwhelms me
and everything has gone.
I face the harsh reality
of hopes and dreams and plans
all abandoned and in ruins.
That which I held fast to
has been wrenched from my grasp
and flung to one side.
I feel the utter despair of
being unable to fulfil
my duties to myself
and others.
There appears to be no solution,
no answer, no way out,
no hope.

It is a point of seeming no return,
yet it is at this time when all my resources
seem to be exhausted,
at this time when I am utterly
weak and cast down
You, mighty God
declare that those who hope in You
will not be disappointed.
When I come to the end of my own
poor resources
I am only at the beginning
of Your limitless riches.

My heart sinks,
but Your Father heart
will never let me fall.

**You take hold of my despair
and give to me the quiet confidence
of Your indwelling spirit.
Beyond my wildest dreams or understanding
You will surely transform the curses
which beset me into blessings.
In the eye of the storm
You assure me
"I am with You".
I know that You will never leave me.
You will answer the unanswerable questions,
the waters will be parted,
the mountain will be moved;
after a season of darkness,
bright skies will come, and
loving Lord
You will surprise me
with Your joy.
Present sorrows will be
replaced with greater blessings.**

*"May the God of hope fill you with all joy and peace
as you trust in him, so that you may overflow with hope
by the power of the Holy Spirit." (Rom. 15.13)*

*"Praise be to the God and Father of our Lord
Jesus Christ! In his great mercy he has given us new
birth into a living hope through the resurrection of
Jesus Christ from the dead..."
(1 Peter 1.3)*

*"Suffering produces perseverance; perseverance,
character; and character; hope. And hope does
not disappoint us, because God has poured out
his love into our hearts by the Holy Spirit,
whom he has given us." (Rom. 5.3-5)*

*"We have this hope as an anchor for the soul."
(Heb. 6.19)*

Defeat

Failure
when success was hoped for,
defeat
when victory seemed assured,
to lose
when winning seemed within grasp,
to have dreams long dreamt
dashed into a myriad of pieces.
All this can rob me of my hope,
my confidence, my vitality, my vision,

Yet the measure of my success or failure
is not in the hands of frail humanity
but in the hands of the One who has bestowed
all gifts and skills, and whose Son
forsook all pedestals, all accolades,
all wealth, prestige and power
and travelled from a lowly manger
to a cruel Cross.

One who knew loneliness, rejection and scorn,
who transformed defeat into glorious victory
and who rose triumphant over His foes.
He was obedient to the Father's will
and He shows now that obedience,
commitment and noble intent
are what God seeks in me,
His creatures He knows so well.

"Take heart! I have overcome the world." (Jn. 16.33)

"With God we shall gain the victory..." (Ps. 60.12)

"Now the prince of this world will be driven out."
(Jn. 12.31)

"Thanks be to God! He gives us the victory through
our Lord Jesus Christ." (1 Cor. 15.57)

"He reached down from on high and took hold of me; He drew me out of deep waters. He rescued me from my powerful enemy, from my foes, who were too strong for me. They confronted me in the day of my disaster, but the Lord was my support. He brought me out into a spacious place; he rescued me because he delighted in me." (Ps. 18.16-19)

"For everyone born of God overcomes the world. This is the victory that has overcome the world, even our faith." (1 John 5.4)

"Now have come the salvation and the power and the kingdom of our God, and the authority of his Christ. For the accuser of our brothers, who accuses them before our God day and night, has been hurled down. They overcame him by the blood of the Lamb and by the word of their testimony; they did not love their lives so much as to shrink from death." (Rev. 12.10-11)

"To him who is able to keep you from falling and to present you before his glorious presence without fault and with great joy – to the only God our Saviour be glory, majesty, power and authority, through Jesus Christ our Lord, before all ages, now and for evermore! Amen." (Jude 24-25)

"The Lord upholds all those who fall and lifts up all who are bowed down." (Ps. 145.14)

Failure

**When pains too heavy to bear
are thrust upon me,
when desolation and despair
overwhelm my frail craft,
when the storm waves
crash over me
and the hammer of adversity
rains blows upon my soul,
when all seems lost
and high hopes are dashed
and brightest dreams are displaced
by malevolent nightmares,
when numbing disaster invades
and all is failure and defeat -
at just this time
I see my Lord alone upon His Cross
and it is at once made clear
that He has walked this path,
that He has known this sorrow,
that His nail-pierced hands hold me
safe and secure,
that at Calvary
He has borne
my sorrows, sins and pain,
conquering death and all adversity
and through His sorrows
will bear me safely
through the darkness and troubled waters
to the glorious dawning of His day.**

*"You will keep in perfect peace him whose mind is steadfast, because he trusts in you."
(Is. 26.3)*

"He calls his own sheep by name..." (Jn 10.3)

Weariness

My pace is slow
my spirit low
the path is rough
the journey long
my strength ebbs out
and footsteps falter.
Life's pilgrim journey
has made me weary.
The road ahead
seems hard and dreary
and in my tiredness
of limb and mind,
with all my energies
drained away,
I hear the kindly,
gentle voice
which bids me come
lay down my load
and rest in Him,
receive His peace
and live again,
rise up renewed,
my strength restored
I stride forth boldly
with my companion
on the way
the One
who is at the beginning
and the end of my long pilgrimage -
the One who is the Way
the Truth
and Life itself.

*"Come to me, all you who are weary and burdened
and I will give you rest." (Matt. 11.28)*

"The Sovereign Lord is my strength; he makes my feet like the feet of a deer, he enables me to go on the heights." (Hab. 3.19)

"Strengthen your feeble arms and weak knees! 'Make level paths for your feet', so that the lame may not be disabled, but rather healed." (Heb. 12.12-13)

"Do you not know? Have you not heard? The Lord is the everlasting God, the Creator of the ends of the earth. He will not grow tired or weary, and his understanding no-one can fathom. He gives strength to the weary and increases the power of the weak…those who hope in the Lord will renew their strength. They will soar on wings like eagles; they will run and not grow weary, they will walk and not be faint." (Is. 40.28-31)

"For to be sure, he was crucified in weakness, yet he lives by God's power. Likewise, we are weak in him, yet by God's power we will live with him to serve you." (2 Cor. 13.4)

"Cast your cares on the Lord and he will sustain you; he will never let the righteous fall." (Ps. 55.22)

Disillusionment

When hopes and dreams of past years
lie shattered
on the bleak landscape of my life,
when high expectations and rich promises
are dashed to the ground,
when heroes, long trusted, are
unmasked, dethroned
and shown to be quite other
than what was thought,
when ideals and beliefs once given
unquestioning commitment
appear to have deep fault lines,
when early enthusiasm
dies away in the face
of the revealed cruelty
and corruption of the world,
at this point I recognise
the disillusionment
which has taken hold of my soul
and a reluctance to be committed or involved
a desire to be an observer not a participant.

The dangers of cynicism and surrender
well up within me, yet in this sorry state
You come and point me
to those values which are
changeless and eternal.

You remind me that the value
of any principle does not depend
upon those who may momentarily support it.
Your revealed truths are not rooted
in passing whims of humanity.

Your light shines brightly in a dark and fallen world
never to be extinguished.
This is not illusion. In this lies my hope.

"When I said, 'My foot is slipping,' your love, O Lord, supported me. When anxiety was great within me, your consolation brought joy to my soul." (Ps. 94.18-19)

"All my longings lie open before you, O Lord: my sighing is not hidden from you." (Ps. 38.9)

"Those who sow in tears will reap with songs of joy." (Ps.126.5)

"The Lord works righteousness and justice for all the oppressed." (Ps. 103.6)

"No matter how many promises God has made, they are 'Yes' in Christ. And so through him the "Amen" is spoken by us to the glory of God." (2 Cor. 1.20)

"Christ in you the hope of glory." (Col. 1.27)

Confusion

The fierce undercurrents
of life
would pull me
in all directions,
one moment
sucking me down
to the depths,
the next
thrusting me up
into dizzying heights,
drawing me
to the one side,
then the other,
removing
all certainty
all fixed points,
driving me
to embrace
the chaotic,
directionless,
uncertainties
of a life
without hope
or purpose,
to loosen my
grip on that
which is secure,
the very anchor
of my soul,
to sweep me away
to where truth
and falsity
are fused,
where good and evil
are so intermingled
that confusion
reigns
in my mind
and soul.

And in these moments
of muddle,
unending
doubt and fear,
You come
and call me
to be still.
You come
and hold me fast
in arms
which are strong
but gentle,
and take me
to the place
where I encounter
that which is real,
sure, dependable and true,
the very Rock of Ages,
the place which is
the unchanging
eternal heart
of a loving
living God,
and my confusion
flees away.

"God is not a God of disorder but of peace."
(1 Cor. 14.33)

"If any of you lacks wisdom, he should ask God, who gives generously to all without finding fault, and it will be given to him." (James 1.5)

"Let us fix our eyes on Jesus, the author and perfecter of our faith..." (Heb. 12.2)

"We will no longer be infants, tossed back and forth by the waves, and blown here and there by every wind of teaching..." (Eph. 4.14)

Guilt

My guilt is as a dark cloud
hovering over me.
I have done so much
I should never have done.
I have said so much
I should never have said.
I have thought so much
I should never have thought.
I have failed
to say, and do and think
that which is good and pure and true.

I am overwhelmed
with feelings of my own unworthiness
of the dark secrets and sins in my life.
My burdens of guilt are cripplingly heavy.

Yet, all-seeing Lord
You know me as I really am,
through and through and, amazingly
in spite of this You love me
and You call me
to return to You.
You long for me
to express my sorrow.
You yearn for me
to repent for what has happened.
You ask me to turn to You
to receive the forgiveness
which cannot be earned
and which I do not deserve.

In the measure that I turn away
from my sins and commit myself
to walk in a new direction
I discover that your mercy holds back
Your judgement on me.
On Your Cross, Lord Jesus,
You carried my burdens of selfishness
and corruption and you come to

forgive me and purify me
from all that is unrighteous.

On the Cross you stop my bleeding.
On the Cross you break the shackles
which have held me down.
You have received my guilt
You set this prisoner free
and Your words to my spirit
are that Your grace is
more than sufficient for all my needs,
now and forever.

"Though your sins are like scarlet, they shall be as white as snow." (Is. 1.18)

"For I will forgive their wickedness and will remember their sins no more." (Jer. 31.34)

"You, O Lord, are a compassionate and gracious God, slow to anger, abounding in love and faithfulness." (Ps. 86.15)

"Out of the depths I cry to you, O Lord; O Lord hear my voice. Let your ears be attentive to my cry for mercy." (Ps. 130.1-2)

"If we confess our sins, he is faithful and just and will forgive us our sins and purify us from all unrighteousness." (1 John 1.9)

"I desire mercy, not sacrifice. For I have not come to call the righteous, but sinners." (Matt. 9.13)

"Create in me a pure heart, O God, and renew a steadfast spirit within me." (Ps. 51.10)

Hurt

I am wounded and the scars
upon my soul are raw
and painful beyond words.
They fiercely sting, penetrating
to the depths of my being.

I do not understand
nor can I fully explain
what is happening.
But when Jesus invites me
to Gethsemane
along the long and tortuous road
to Calvary
I hear the tumult and the cruel cries.

I begin, in some small measure
to see that You chose to bear it all for me.
The purpose of Your redemptive suffering
is at last made clear
and You transform
all my hurts into blessings.
You bind up all my wounds
You bring me Your peace.

"'Because he loves me,' says the Lord, 'I will rescue him; I will protect him, for he acknowledges my name. He will call upon me, and I will answer him; I will be with him in trouble, I will deliver him and honour him'."
(Ps. 91.14-15)

"I am in pain and distress; may your salvation, O God, protect me." (Ps. 69.29)

"In my distress I called to the Lord, and he answered me." (Jonah 2.2)

Regret

I look back
with sadness
pain and guilt
as I recall
things I have done
which I should never have done,
things I have said
which I should never have said.

As I recall
their significance
I am filled with remorse,
frustration and regret
and realise I cannot undo
what has been done.
I cannot unsay
what has been said.

My unease and sadness
is still further fuelled
when I recall those times
when I did not do
what I ought to have done
and I did not say
what I ought to have said.

The tide of time
has flowed swiftly on
and I know that
I cannot buy back
past words and deeds and silences
and the memory of them
causes deep regret and hurt
which recurs over the years
of my life, continuing to influence
my moods, my judgements
my lifestyle,
continuing to burden me with guilt
continuing to rob me of joy.

I nostalgically
cling on to old pains
which become heavier burdens
of guilt and remorse
from which there seems no escape
and the fingers of the clock
steadfastly refuse to be pushed back.
I continue to feel the wounds of long ago,
the past overshadows me,
invades and even controls me.

There seems no escape
yet the only one
who sees, who knows
and shares my regrets
is the one who can free me from them all.
He, our kindly Maker,
the Lord of all the years
is not the captive of time.
For Him past years and now are one.
His healing spans all time,
all memory.

He, who changes not,
comes and pours the waters of His Spirit
to wash away every stain of the past,
comes in the fire of the Spirit
to burn away the rubbish of the past,
and comes to shed the light of His Spirit
upon the darkest corners of my life.

As the Divine Potter He claims
the soft clay of my life
and moulds it into something beautiful.
He fashions me to be Christ-like
and He holds me, gently
in the palms of His hands,
expelling the ghosts and flaws of the past
and preparing me for heaven.

"Forget the former things; do not dwell on the past. See I am doing a new thing!...I am making a way in the desert..." (Is. 43.18-19)

"The glory of this present house will be greater than the glory of the former house." (Haggai 2.9)

"Forgetting what is behind...I press on towards the goal..." (Phil 3.13-14)

"I will repay you for the years the locusts have eaten." (Joel 2.25)

"If anyone is in Christ, he is a new creation; the old has gone, the new has come!" (2 Cor. 5.17)

"Godly sorrow brings repentance that leads to salvation and leaves no regret, but worldly sorrow brings death." (2 Cor. 7.10)

"He who was seated on the throne said, ' I am making everything new!' Then he said, 'Write this down, for these words are trustworthy and true'." (Rev. 21.5)

"In all things God works for the good of those who love him, who have been called according to his purpose." (Rom. 8.28)

Doubt

There comes a time
when nothing seems sure,
nothing seems true,
nothing seems real.
A time when all certainties
are questioned.
Is everything I believe
an illusion?
Have I been living
a lie?

When doubts assail me
I am tempted to abandon
all faith, all certainty.
A doubting, unbelieving
cynical and critical world
invades my soul
and worldly voices tell me
it is better to be uncommitted,
to drift, not to commit myself to anything.

Yet deep down
I know this to be negation
and life-denying.
Each period of doubt in my life
is a dark cloud
hovering over me,
a dank fog choking me.

But the one who has given me
great gifts of faith
and hope and love
has also given me
a questioning mind,
a deep desire to embrace
the truth.
And so through questions,
fears, suspicions
I can experience with new freshness
the revelation of God Himself

who knows moment by moment
how I feel
and all that is on my mind.

He wants my honesty,
my openness,
my readiness
to explore new truths.
He would have me turn away
from all murmurings
and siren sounds,
from mockers and cynics,
and lead me gently
to the rock upon which
I can depend.
He builds me up,
He is the encourager,
His hand is strong,
He enables me to believe
and helps my unbelief.
He rescues me
from sterile human reasoning
to explore,
with exhilarating freedom
and wild expectation,
the wonders of the Lord of surprises.

And in all this
He sets me free
from my inward lookingness
to behold His glory.

"Faith is being sure of what we hope for and certain of what we do not see." (Heb. 11.1)

"I do believe; help me overcome my unbelief." (Mk. 9.24)

Rejection

You were done to death
outside the city wall
You were excluded
from the presence
of the rich and powerful.
You knew what it was
to be despised
and rejected.
You knew the cry of the mob - 'Crucify Him!'
And forever more
You stand with the
poor and persecuted,
the untouchables,
the outcast and excluded.
You are close to the scapegoats
and misfits.
Those who walk with You
do not know
the supposed comfort
and safety of the crowd.
They do not conform.
They do not bow down
to false gods.
They do not buy into
easy compromise
and are not burnt up
with bitter anger
in the desert
of apartness.
In my rejection
I have the opportunity
of meeting and sharing
with the one
who is the Saviour of the world
and who embraces me
as a friend and even brother -
the lover of my soul.

"Many of his disciples turned back and no longer went about with him. So Jesus asked the twelve 'Do you also wish to go away?' Simon Peter answered him, 'Lord to whom can we go? You have the words of eternal life. We have come to believe and know that you are the Holy One of God'."
(John 6.66-69) NRSV

"The Lord is close to the broken-hearted and saves those who are crushed in spirit." (Ps. 34.18)

"He was despised and rejected by men..."
(Is. 53.3)

"The Lord is a refuge for the oppressed, a stronghold in times of trouble." (Ps. 9.9)

"God has said 'Never will I leave you; never will I forsake you'." (Heb. 13.5)

"The Lord is my shepherd, I shall not be in want."
(Ps. 23.1)

"The stone the builders rejected has become the capstone..." (Ps. 118.22)

"The Son of Man must suffer many things and be rejected…" (Lk. 9.22)

"Though my father and mother forsake me, the Lord will receive me." (Ps. 27.10)

Lostness

Each one of us
was born.
Each one of us
will surely pass away.
Death is a reminder
of our frail humanity.
Our residence
in this world
is temporary, impermanent,
but death
is a parting,
often painful,
filled with sadness
always beyond
our full understanding.

You give me
the precious gift of mourning
and in this process
of remembering and rejoicing
in the wonder
of a precious life
I am led from sorrow
into dancing.
The dark shadows
are gently put on one side
and I am bathed in
the glorious light
of Your continuing presence
- You who are the Lord
of life and death.

As I ponder
on the unsearchable
mystery of death,
Lord show to me
the fragility of life.
Affirm within me
the sure promise of
eternal life

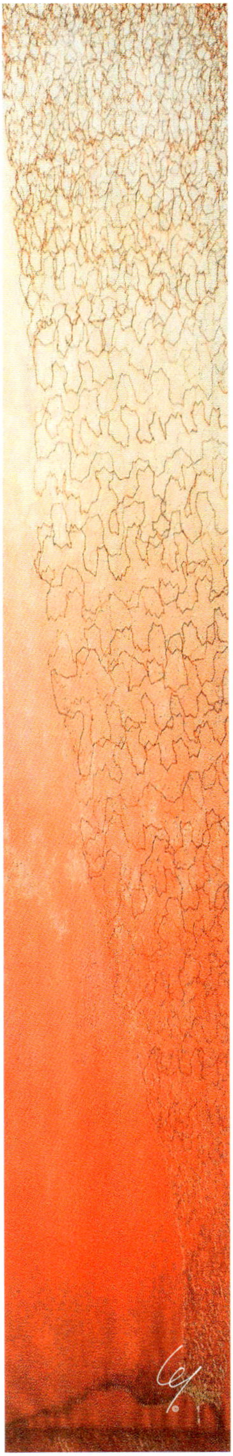

which You have offered to me.
Help me not to live a lie
as though I should never,
ever die.
Help me to receive
from You
the gift of life with You.
Help me not forever
to play with illusions
doubts and fears
and while away my life.

Help me in this world,
as I receive Your Spirit of life,
to live abundantly,
comforting and being comforted,
giving and receiving,
blessing and being blessed,
forgiving and being forgiven,
constantly assured
that sorrow and sighing
will flee away,
constantly assured
that there is
real purpose
and immense value
in our frail humanity.

In a dying world
may I constantly
spring to life
in resurrection joy.
He has died
but He is risen
and He will come again.

"In quietness and trust is your strength..." (Is. 30.15)

"You are my hiding-place; you will protect me from trouble and surround me with songs of deliverance." (Ps. 32.7)

"Whether you turn to the right or to the left, your ears will hear a voice behind you, saying, 'This is the way; walk in it'." (Is. 30.21)

"Your word is a lamp to my feet
and a light for my path." (Ps. 119.105)

"When my spirit grows faint within me, it is you who know my way." (Ps. 142.3)

"I have come that they may have life,
and have it to the full." (Jn. 10.10)

"God has given us eternal life, and this life is in his Son." (1 Jn. 5.11)

"Your Father in heaven is not willing that any of these little ones should be lost." (Matt. 18.14)

"Then he calls his friends and neighbours together and says, 'Rejoice with me; I have found my lost sheep'." (Lk. 15.6)

"I am the way and the truth and the life." (Jn. 14.6)

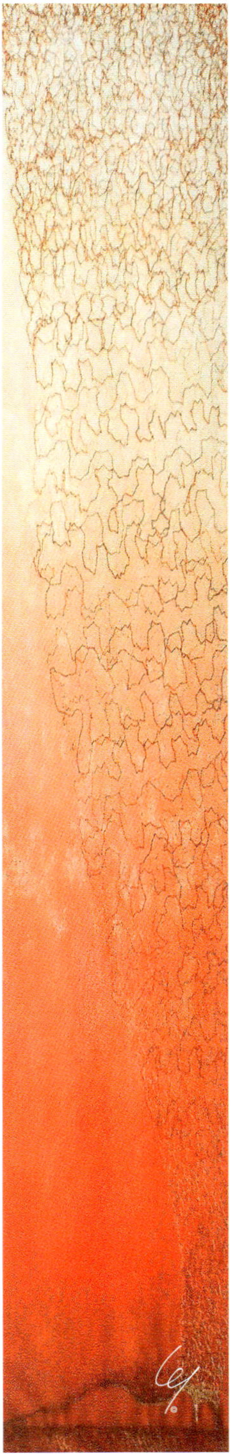

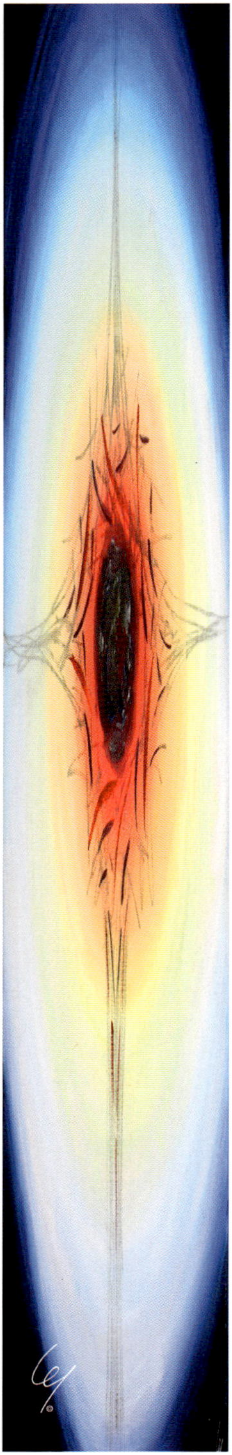

Pain

Unease, discomfort
and pain within me
may be
a momentary reminder
or an insistent warning
of the needs
of my body or mind.
The system of my senses
is yet another sign that I am
fearfully and wonderfully made
and for this I thank you Lord.

A continuing
persistent and protracted agony
may become a burden to me
distasteful and crippling
and I long for its removal.
Its relentless intensity
exceeds my understanding
and I struggle
to accommodate it within me,
giving me agony of body and soul.
I may cry out -'Why Lord?'

The Lord may not come
to explain it,
but He most certainly
will come to share it.

Forgive my frustration
when I fail to understand its meaning.
It may become an unwelcome
guest within me,
yet I discover
I can say in truth
You are with me,
You are the One
who shares with me
and bears with me.
You are the One
who comforts my distress.

You are the One
who on Your Cross
bears all the pains and sorrows
of a sinful world,
redeeming, purifying, blessing.

If I remain close to You
with all my frustration and unease
You will show me
that in sickness and in health
my life has great purpose
and is of limitless value.

You understand all
about pain and sickness,
disease and disorder
in this our fallen world.
In giving these to You
and sharing them with You
You introduce me to the mystery of healing.
You reveal Your miraculous power
to save and cure,
Your power to put right what is wrong,
to transform the ugly
into something beautiful - for You.
You show me that all things
without exception
work together for good
to all who love You.

I may not understand
the cause and meaning of my pain
because I see
through a glass darkly,
but in Your good time
You will reveal to me
Your ways
and I will know
the joy and gladness
of Your children
and I will know that in You
all sorrow and pain
will flee away.

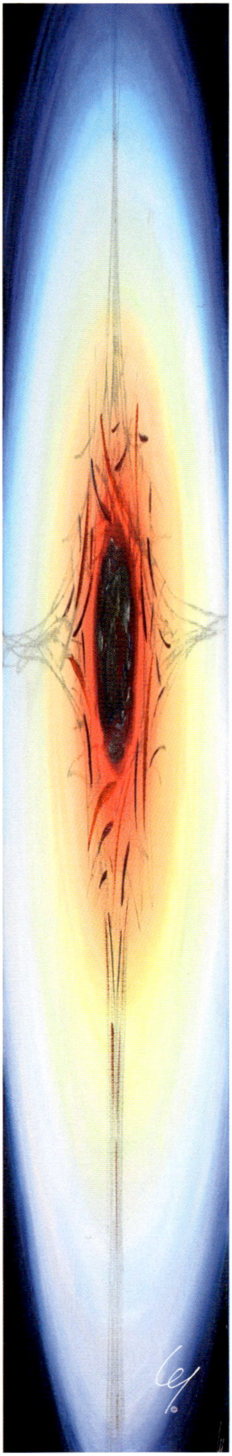

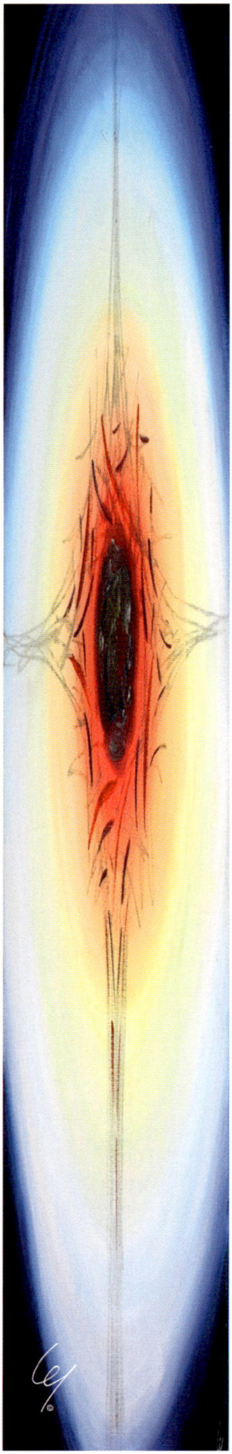

"The righteous cry out, and the Lord hears them; he delivers them from all their troubles."
(Ps. 34.17)

"He heals the broken-hearted and binds up their wounds." (Ps. 147.3)

"The Lord will rescue me from every evil attack and will bring me safely to his heavenly kingdom."
(2 Tim. 4.18)

"Look upon my suffering and deliver me…Defend my cause and redeem me; preserve my life according to your promise."
(Ps. 119.153-154)

"The Lord watches over you..The Lord will keep you from all harm – he will watch over your life..."
(Ps. 121.5-7)

"For he will command his angels concerning you to guard you in all your ways; they will lift you up in their hands, so that you will not strike your foot against a stone."
(Ps 91.11-12)

"For my yoke is easy and my burden is light."
(Matt. 11.30)

Sickness

My sickness robs me
of my time,
my freedom, my comfort and my joy.
It is a burden
I do not wish
to carry.

My yearning is for liberation.

My disorders,
which cause me such discomfort and distress,
I do not understand.
I cannot explain
that from the depths of my being
I seek wholeness
and healing,
I seek well-being
and deep within me
I know that my wounded body
my troubled mind
my hurting heart
cannot in fullness be transformed
save by my Father,
the lover of my soul
and by His Son
the bearer of my pains and sorrows,
my wounded Healer.

To Him I give my sickness and disease,
to Him I offer up my life
to Him I turn in time of need
in the sure and certain knowledge
that His touch, today as ever
brings peace and healing
brings purpose to my illness
brings joy and deliverance to my whole being
and with His strength I overcome

and all is well and all will be well.

"Hear my prayer, O Lord; let my cry for help come to you…my bones burn… my heart is blighted….. I lie awake… He will respond to the prayer of the destitute; he will not despise their plea."
(Ps. 102. 1,3,4,7,17)

"I am the Lord, who heals you." (Ex. 15.26)

"By His wounds we are healed." (Is. 53.5)

"Praise the Lord, O my soul, and forget not all his benefits – who forgives all your sins and heals all your diseases, who redeems your life from the pit and crowns you with love and compassion."
(Ps. 103.2-4)

"He sent forth his word and healed them..."
(Ps. 107.20)

"People brought to him all who were ill from various diseases… and he healed them."
(Matt. 4.24)

"Do you want to get well?" (Jn. 5.6)

"Lord I do not deserve to have you come under my roof. But just say the word, and my servant will be healed." (Matt. 8.8)

"I call on the Lord in my distress, and he answers me." (Ps. 120.1)

"May your unfailing love be my comfort, according to your promise to your servant."
(Ps. 119.76)

"I will turn their mourning into gladness; I will give them comfort and joy instead of sorrow."
(Jer. 31.13)

Incapacity

For reasons
far beyond my understanding
I may carry
throughout my life
limitations
on what I can do,
on what I can hear or see,
on where I can go.

I may know the frustration
of being held back,
limited and restrained.

I may experience
outrage and injustice,
pain, fear and loneliness.

But when I allow
the one
who is called
'the Man of Sorrows'
into my every experience
He will present to me
the amazing
the unbelievable
the outrageous
gift of abundant life.

He will release in me
new songs
new joys
new discoveries.
He will transform
every situation.
He will liberate me
in all my limitations
and will overwhelm those
who believe themselves
to be free.

The stale, fruitless struggle
to understand why I am, how I am,
will be displaced
by the glorious, fresh struggle
to explore, and to discover.

Not by my power
but through the grace of God
I will do the impossible
I will scale mountains
I will fly like a bird,
the wind of the Spirit
will fill my sails
and there will be laughter
on earth as there is in heaven.

"'My grace is sufficient for you, for my power is made perfect in weakness'. Therefore I will boast all the more gladly about my weaknesses, so that Christ's power may rest on me."
(2 Cor. 12.9)

"Nothing is impossible with God." (Lk. 1.37)

"The Lord gives strength to his people." (Ps. 29.11)

"You brought my life up from the pit."
(Jonah 2.6)

"The eternal God is your refuge and underneath are the everlasting arms." (Deut. 33.27)

"To bestow on them a crown of beauty instead of ashes, the oil of gladness instead of mourning, and a garment of praise instead of a spirit of despair."
(Is. 61.3)

"I have loved you with an everlasting love; I have drawn you with loving-kindness. I will build you up again..." (Jer. 31.3-4)

Betrayal

When promises are broken
discarded and forgotten,
when friends
betray,
when trust
is shattered
into a thousand pieces,
when agreements are reneged on
and bonds of seeming integrity broken,
my soul is pierced
with sadness, anger
and disbelief.
When those in whom I placed
my confidence, my hope, my trust
plunge a knife into my soul,
I do not understand
and my hurt is unassuaged,
until
I recall that My Lord
was despised,
was rejected,
was betrayed,
and then I know that I can walk
in His footsteps
in the sure and certain knowledge
that He is trustworthy,
He is faithful,
His love
will never grow cold.

The darkness of
unkindness, corruption and greed
can never extinguish His light
which sets me free
from all sense of injustice
because the heavenly Father is just,
He is unchanging
and His mercy continues for ever.

*"Even my close friend, whom I trusted, he who shared my bread, has lifted up his heel against me.
But you, O Lord, have mercy on me..."
(Ps. 41.9,10)*

"Trust in the Lord with all your heart and lean not on your own understanding..." (Prov. 3.5)

"Look, the hour is near, and the Son of Man is betrayed into the hands of sinners." (Matt. 26.45)

"Father, forgive them, for they do not know what they are doing." (Lk. 23.34)

*"I will exalt you, O Lord, for you lifted me out of the depths and did not let my enemies gloat over me.
O Lord my God, I called to you for help and you healed me." (Ps. 30.1-2)*

Desolation

When I am
cast down
there seems
no way
to rise.

I have fallen
to a dark depth
of despair
and defeat.

There seems
no way
to escape
my dark moods
which hem me in.

No one
seems to understand
or even care.

Self-doubt
and hopelessness
pervade my soul.

Yet as I cry
out of the depths
of defeat
and hopelessness
my Lord
comes down
into my pit
to share the mire
of my squalor
and gently, silently
lifts me up
in His strong hands
out of the damp depths
to which I have sunk.

With Him
I begin to breathe pure air.
I feel the sun and breeze
upon my face.
I am filled with hope
and emptied of all fear
I am at once set free.
I begin
to understand
resurrection joy.

"Why are you downcast, O my soul? Why so disturbed within me? Put your hope in God..."
(Ps. 43.5)

"I have summoned you by name; you are mine."
(Is. 43.1)

"The Lord is faithful, and he will strengthen and protect you from the evil one." (2 Thess. 3.3)

"Because you are my help, I sing in the shadow of your wings. My soul clings to you; your right hand upholds me." (Ps. 63.7,8)

"'Though the mountains be shaken and the hills be removed, yet my unfailing love for you will not be shaken nor my covenant of peace be removed', says the Lord, who has compassion on you."
(Is. 54.10)

Loneliness

When I am alone
I may know
the purity, the peace
and the stillness of God
deeply pervading my separation
from the wider world
and bringing me peace.

Yet my aloneness
may become my loneliness
with deep and often unfulfilled
desire for fellowship
or closeness with another,
the sharing and caring
in the spirit.

Then the Lord comes and offers
the most intimate relationship,
the deepest sharing, with Him
and also with His people.
Thus the Lord
banishes all the pain
of loneliness.
I am truly and fully alive
when I am alone with God
who sees all,
knows all,
and is all-loving.

*"I am with you and will watch over you
wherever you go..." (Gen. 28.15)*

*"Neither death nor life, neither angels nor demons,
neither the present nor the future, nor any powers,
neither height nor depth, nor anything else in all
creation, will be able to separate us from the love of
God that is in Christ Jesus our Lord." (Rom.8.38-39)*

Depression

I am a creature of moods
and feelings
which come and go
and rise and fall.
I blow hot and cold.
Just as the recollection
of all that is good and
beautiful in my mind
leads me to a pinnacle of elation,
so the recollection
of all the dark things
leads me to the depths
of desolation and depression
from which, so often in vain,
I try to escape.
I am dragged down and anchored
to thoughts and visions
which are full of gloom
sadness and despair.
Yet if I go to the heights
or the depths
I know You are there.
I know I cannot drift
beyond Your love and care.
I know Your arms
will bear me up.
I know the heavy chains
which rob me of my freedom,
will be broken
and I can hear You say to my soul
'Be still, I the Lord am with you',
ever living,
ever present,
ever loving.

"You will rejoice, and no-one will take away your joy."
(Jn. 16.22)

The Promise

You never promised
I would not go through fire,
I would not go through the raging waters,
I would not go through conflicts and battlefields.

But You have promised
I will not be burnt,
I will not be drowned,
I will be victorious,

because You
the Mighty One
are with me

and will never let me go.

"Cast all your anxiety on him because he cares for you." (1 Peter 5.7)

"Even though I walk through the valley of the shadow of death, I will fear no evil, for you are with me; your rod and your staff, they comfort me." (Ps. 23.4)

"The Spirit of the Lord is on me because he has anointed me to preach good news to the poor.
He has sent me to proclaim freedom
for the prisoners and recovery of sight for the blind,
to release the oppressed, to proclaim
the year of the Lord's favour." (Lk. 4.18-19)

"I have come that they may have life, and have it to the full." (Jn. 10.10)

"Peace I leave with you; my peace I give you.
I do not give to you as the world gives.
Do not let your hearts be troubled and
do not be afraid." (Jn.14.27)

The Vision

Tears will be wiped away
Sorrow will be turned into joy
The blind will see
The deaf will hear
The dumb will speak
The lame will walk
The sick will be healed
The hungry will be fed
The dead will live
The desert will bloom
Dry bones will spring to life
Broken walls will be rebuilt
Prisoners will be set free
The crooked will be made straight
Light will burst into our darkness
God's glory will be revealed.

"..in Christ all will be made alive." (1 Cor. 15.22)

"I can do everything through him who gives me strength." (Phil. 4.13)

"The zeal of the Lord Almighty will accomplish this." (Is. 9.7)

"Come, Lord Jesus." (Rev. 22.20)

"I pray that you, being rooted and established in love, may have power, together with all the saints, to grasp how wide and long and high and deep is the love of Christ, and to know this love that surpasses knowledge – that you may be filled to the measure of all the fullness of God." (Eph. 3.17-19)

Complete Healing

"Then the angel showed me the river of the water of life, as clear as crystal,
flowing from the throne of God
and of the Lamb
down the middle of the great street of the city.

On each side of the river stood the tree of life,
bearing twelve crops of fruit,
yielding its fruit every month.

And the leaves of the tree are
for the healing of the nations.

No longer will there be any curse.

The throne of God and of the Lamb
will be in the city,
and his servants will serve him.
They will see his face, and his name
will be on their foreheads.

There will be no more night.
They will not need the light of a lamp
or the light of the sun,
for the Lord God will give them light.
And they will reign for ever and ever."
(Rev. 22.1-5)

"Then will the eyes of the blind be opened and the ears of the deaf unstopped. Then will the lame leap like a deer, and the mute tongue shout for joy…. Gladness and joy will overtake them, and sorrow and sighing will flee away."
(Is. 35.5,6,10)

"The Lord will be your everlasting light,
and your God will be your glory."
(Is. 60.19)

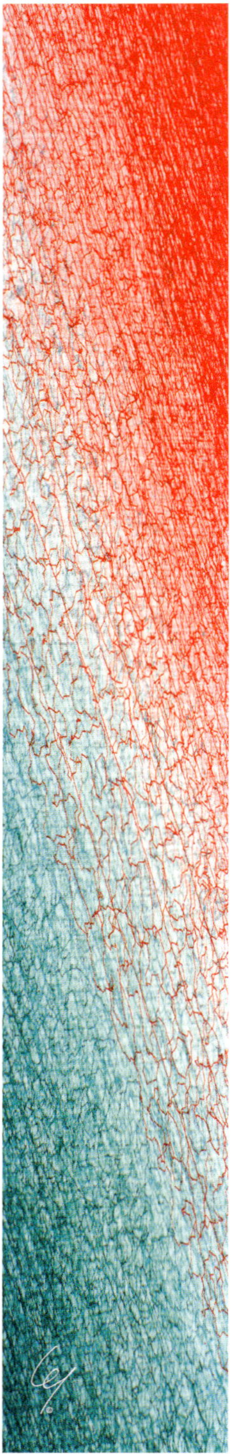

Here in the maddening maze of things
When tossed by storm and flood
To one fixed ground my spirit clings;
I know that God is good…

William Cowper

When darkness intercepts the skies,
And sorrow's waves around me roll,
When high the storms of passion rise,
And half o'erwhelm my sinking soul,
My soul a sudden calm shall feel,
And hear a whisper, "Peace; be still!"

Charles Wesley

So long Your power has blest me,
sure it still will lead me on
o'er moor and fen, o'er crag and torrent,
till the night is gone.

John Henry Newman

Though waves and storms go o'er my head,
Though strength, and health, and friends be gone,
Though joys be withered all and dead,
Though every comfort be withdrawn,
On this my steadfast soul relies-
Father, Your mercy never dies!

John Wesley

I delivered you when bound
and when bleeding healed your wound
sought you wandering,
set you right
turned your darkness into light.

William Cowper

If you place that which is ugly
on the altar of God,
He will transform it into
something beautiful for Him.

Mother Teresa of Calcutta

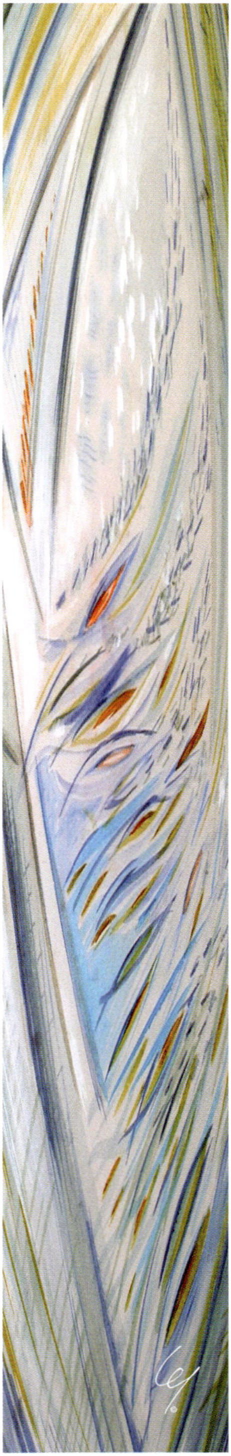

The Maranatha Community is a movement of thousands of
Christians who are active in churches of all denominations
throughout the United Kingdom and overseas. It is committed
to praying and working for Christian Unity,
Christian Healing and Christian Renewal.
It is a servant ministry of prayer and action.

Dennis Wrigley, the author, is the Co-Founder and Leader
of the Maranatha Community which was formed 30 years ago.
His previous books have included 'One Lord, One People',
'Encounter with God', 'The Cross of Christ'
and jointly with Sister Elizabeth Tuttle 'Walking with God'.

The Maranatha Community
102 Irlam Road, Flixton, Manchester M41 6JT
Tel: 0161 748 4858 Fax: 0161 747 7379
www.maranathacommunity.org.uk
email: info@maranathacommunity.org.uk